Sociocracy For All is a nonprofit operating globally and registered in Massachusetts, USA. www.sociocracyforall.org
All content is licensed under a CC-SA-BY-NC license. 2023
ISBN: 978-1-949183-12-2
Ted Rau (2023). Sociocracy. A brief introduction. Sociocracy For All

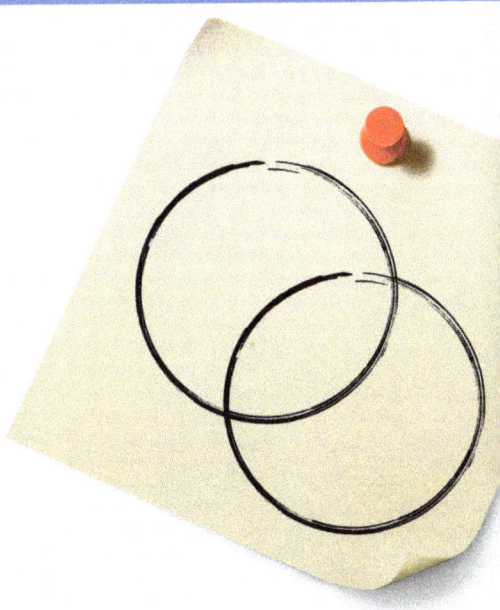

Table of contents

Introduction	x
Making group decisions: consent	1
Who decides what: circles and roles	11
The sociocratic selection process	21
Meetings with sociocracy	31
Creating clarity with co-created proposals	43
Feedback and improvement	53
Learning more	66

Introduction

Human societies follow rulesets that have been passed down to us for a long time. The rules tell us that's it's normal that some have power and resources, and that others don't. To so many, this is not the game they want to play anymore. Now what? Most of us never learned any other game.

Sociocracy is such a rule set for organizations, and it offers a way out of the power games. It consists of

- an inclusive and effective way of making decisions
- distributed and transparent leadership in circles and roles
- clear connecting ways to structure our meetings.

Sociocracy goes way beyond majority vote or endless large group processes. It adds transparency, ease, and flow.

This book is meant as a first overview, with links on how to learn more.

    Enjoy!

Ted

Making consent decisions

Why consent decision-making?

We all know different decision-making methods:

- autocratic decisions: one person decides
- majority vote: the majority decides
- consensus: everyone agrees

Most groups use a mix of all those decision-making methods in their meetings.

Consent is the default decision-making method in sociocracy. **Consent** is the most similar to consensus decision-making*.

*Depending on how consensus is interpreted and practiced, it might even look the same.

Autocratic decisions
- 😀 clear authority
- 😀 fast decisions possible
- 😐 loses a lot of information
- 😐 likely not a lot of buy-in

Majority vote
- 😀 easy to do with many people
- 😀 hears the majority
- 😐 ignores minority needs
- 😐 polarizes decisions

Consensus
- 😀 every voice counts
- 😀 lots of conversation
- 😐 can take a long time

What is consent?

what you want
(preference)

what you can work with
(range of tolerance)

} consent

what you cannot work with
(objection = proposal is in conflict with the aim)

— objection

Let's say a group wants to solve a problem and there are different options to choose from. Typically, every group member will have a preference. Yet, in a group, we would not be able to make decisions if everyone insisted on getting their first choice. So we widen our options to also include things that are within our range of tolerance.

No objection from a circle member can be ignored. When there are objections, we need to tweak the proposal more. Consent on a proposal is reached when everyone says that they can at least work with the proposal.

Aims and the range of tolerance

The work we do together, our aim, is the backdrop to evaluate what 'works' and what doesn't.

For example, if our circle's aim is "running a concert venue" then any decision that violates fire safety and risks us losing our ability to hold events would be a proposal we would have to object to.

This shows you how important it is to have an agreed-upon aim so we can decide what decisions are acceptable - otherwise, people would always just decide based on their preferences.

Objections

Here is the surprising thing about consent decision-making: objections are not a "bad" thing anymore. Quite the opposite: objections are what helps us make proposals better and align with our aim.

Since supporting the aim is ultimately what we want, objections will be celebrated!

No one can block a decision just because they don't like it. If someone objects, the circle will want to hear the reasons and how the proposal is in conflict with the aim so they can improve the proposal.

Every circle member can object, and only when all objections have been integrated (see page 9) can a decision move forward.

It's important to know that people outside the circle can be heard and give feedback but will not be able to object to a decision. The idea is that a circle has all the people as members who know the circle's work well, who are involved in the work related to the circle.

The consent process

To make a decision, we follow 3 easy steps to make sure everyone is on the same page and there are no misunderstandings.

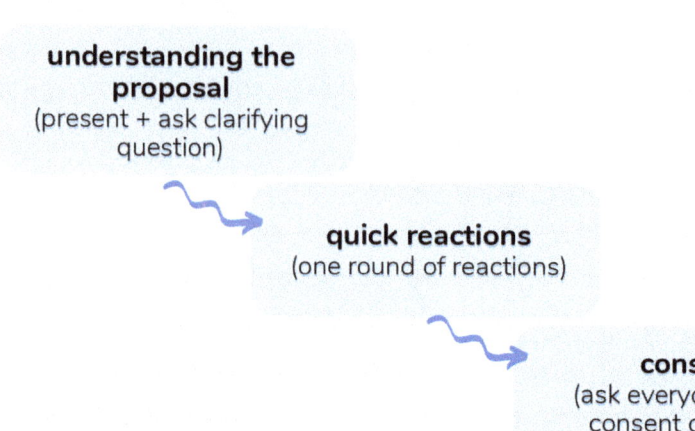

① Understanding the proposal

This step is easy: read the proposal out loud and allow everyone to ask their questions about the proposal — ideally only clarifying questions to understand the proposal as intended, no suggestive questions.
If there are a lot of questions, you can have people ask their questions in a round.
Answer as many questions as you can, then go to the next step.

② Quick reactions

Next, give everyone a chance to say what they think about the proposal. Ideally, you do this in a round — that way, you can be sure everyone has actually been heard.

People might share how they feel about the proposal, or they might express other ideas they have. One round is typically enough.

After the reaction round, you have the opportunity to amend the proposal. The facilitator can also ask the author, circle leader or any other person to restate an amended proposal.

> Note: watch out, this is where group process can easily get chaotic, especially if there are a lot of ideas.
> Slow down and trust the facilitator's judgement of what suggestions to include - too many cooks can spoil the broth!

③ Consent

It's the moment of decision! Now we hear from each person whether they consent or object to the proposal.

They will consent if they think the proposal is good enough for now (or safe enough to try). And they will object if they are convinced that the proposal brings negative results that will keep the circle from achieving its aim.

And if you neither love the proposal nor do you have an objection? Then you consent - consent means not having an objection.

A quick way is to ask for thumbs up/down but a safer way is to do a whole round.

In consent decision-making, there is no room for abstentions or concerns that aren't objections. If someone has a concern, encourage them to object. Objections aren't anything to avoid, and whatever someone might be concerned about might contain important information.

(This is important because too many groups have experienced toxic group dynamics when someone consents but was actually concerned — it is likely that they will complain later.)

Integrating objections

Objections are the safety net that ensures that proposals are actually good enough.

So how can we harvest the wisdom they bring in a time-effective way?

Sociocracy offers three main stra-tegies of integrating objections, and often they get combined.

Modify the proposal
What in the proposal can you change to avoid the negative effect?

Shorten the term
Can you try the proposal out for a short(er) period of time to see what happens?

Measure the concern
Can you try out the proposal and make an agreement on what you will track that would indicate negative implications?

Tips and tricks

The most typical mistake is to stop in the reaction round and to hear reactions, and reactions, ... and reactions, instead of moving to the next step of hearing consent/objections. Much too often, we tweak a proposal that is already good enough and get lost - just because we don't dare to ask for consent.

Another common point that can lead to friction is if the facilitator or the participants mix questions, reactions and consent/objections. If everyone is on a different step, it becomes much less likely that people listen to each other.

Another note; after the reaction round, even if there were additional ideas, it's totally fine to still keep the proposal the same. What counts at the end is whether there are objections. Sometimes, it actually complicates the process to accommodate all additional ideas. Also, not every concern rises to an objection.

Tips and tricks

Decisions in sociocracy are made in circles; each circle makes its own decisions. Circles typically have 4-8 members.

How do we know what decision is made by which circle? We know that because we define what circle has what domain as part of our circle structure. Then, every circle is able to make decisions in its domain autonomously, which means without having to ask anyone else.

Each circle also has an aim: a description of what the circle does. The aim and the domain come as a package deal: you get responsibility and authority together, so that those who do the work in that domain also have the authority to act.

Circle roles

To run effectively, each circle will select who will fill which of these roles:

- Leader - oversees operations and makes sure the circle works towards its aim.
- Facilitator - moderates the meetings
- Secretary - takes notes during meetings and makes sure the circle documents are up to date.
- Delegate - represents the circle's voice in the next-higher circle.

It's not uncommon to hold several roles at once. For example, the same person can be leader and secretary; this is up to the circle and its members and can change over time.

Groups sometimes rename the roles; for example, leader as (internal) coordinator or focalizer; facilitator as moderator; secretary as admin or scribe; delegate as representative or external coordinator.

Linking

Leaders and delegates are linking roles.
This means they are connectors to the parent or 'next-higher' circle.

That means that two people will be members of both circles. They will carry information from one circle to another, and back, and make sure that decisions are aligned — since they are full members, their consent is needed in the parent circle to move forward.

The leader is often seen as the top-down link, and the delegate as the bottom-up link.

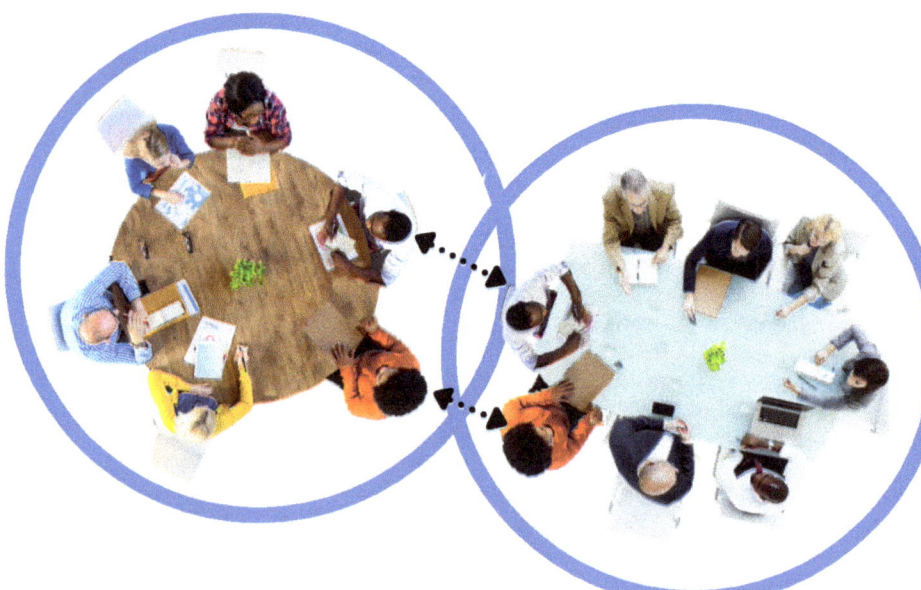

The General Circle

At the very center of the organization is the General Circle (GC). The GC consists *only* of linking roles: leaders of all department circles and their delegates.

The aim of the GC is to make sure all department circles have what they need to function and that all aims and domains are clear and we always know what gets decided where.

That means that the GC only decides who decides - but the decisions connected to our work are exclusively made in the circles themselves to keep decisions decentralized. The GC cannot override a circle's decision.

Sociocracy For All

Circle structure

The whole system of nested circles and linked roles creates a structure where...

- It's clear where decisions are made - and circles are autonomous in decisions in their domains.
- Information flows between circles through linking and operational handoffs.
- Circles are aligned with each other through the links' consent.
- Every circle is embedded in its support system.
- The circle system can grow and adapt where more energy is needed.

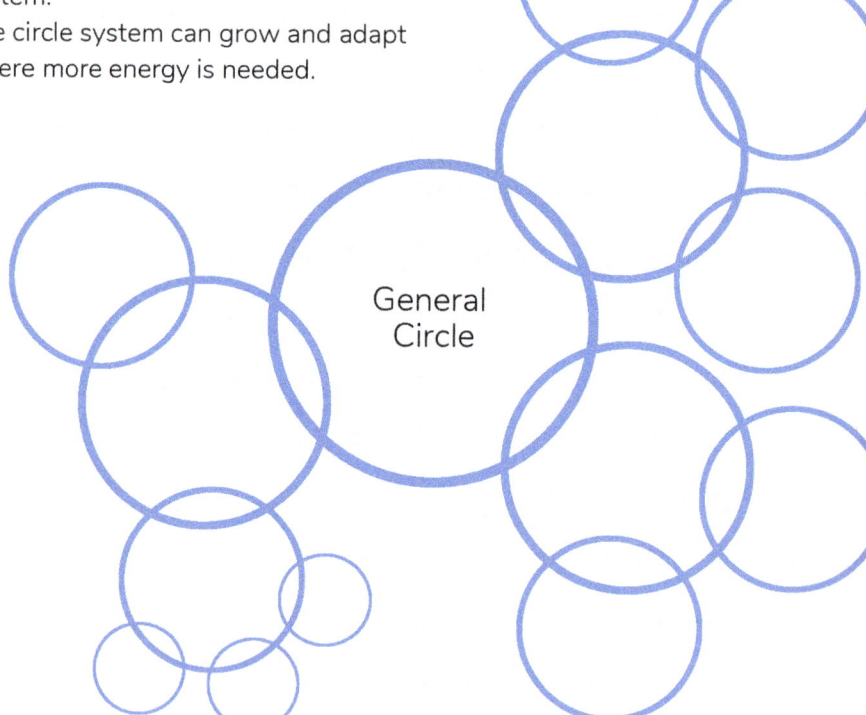

General Circle

Operational roles

Circles oversee operations in their domain. The work is typically done by the circle members.

To further differentiate who does what in a circle, a circle can form operational roles. The role is created with circle consent to the role description that describes which activities are clustered in the role. Then the circle selects someone to fill the role.

For example, a Social Media Circle might make decisions on the social media strategy together but then create roles for each social media platform where individual circle members then carry out their work (posting, creating social media images, etc.) in alignment with those agreements and workflows.

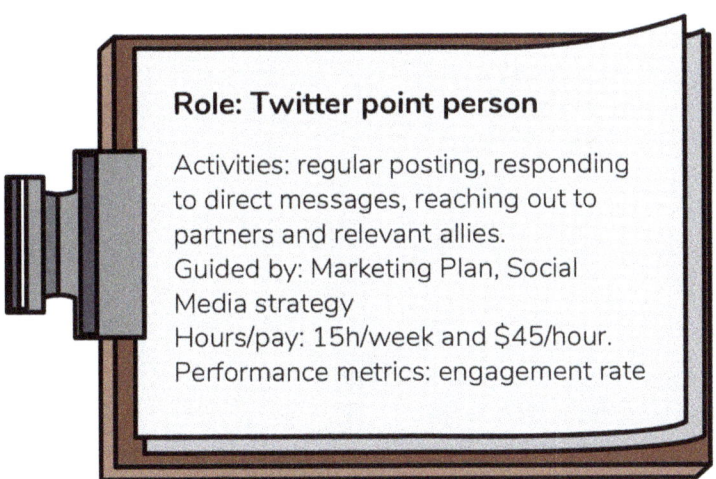

Role: Twitter point person

Activities: regular posting, responding to direct messages, reaching out to partners and relevant allies.
Guided by: Marketing Plan, Social Media strategy
Hours/pay: 15h/week and $45/hour.
Performance metrics: engagement rate

It's common for an individual to hold several roles at once. For example, a member of an organization might be in two circles: Marketing and Social Media Circle. This person might be the leader of Social Media Circle, hold the operational role of the Twitter point person in Social Media Circle, and be the facilitator of Marketing Circle - a mix of (process-oriented) circle roles and operational roles.

Information flow + feedback

Remember that decisions are decentralized in sociocracy!
For example, it's well possible that the Membership Circle might be a sub-sub-circle and still has the power to set the membership fee for everyone in the organization.

The reason this works is because of the clear pattern of aims and domains that give very defined "pieces" of authority and responsibility to clearly defined groups. Another factor is that the decisions are not made by a random circle but by the circle of people who do the work related to that circle.

However, each circle is responsible not only for the work and well-being in its own domain but also for getting feedback from the rest of the organization so that decisions made in the circle align well with the other decisions in other circles and support everyone in the organization in their work.

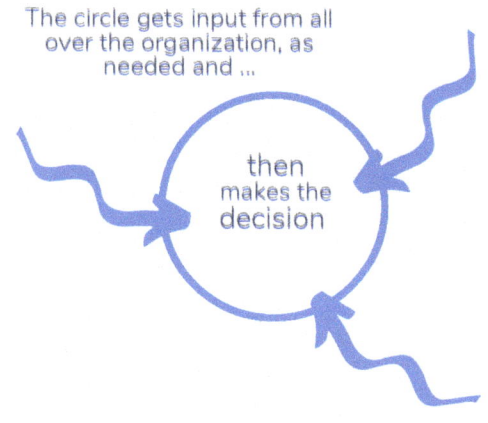

One can hear feedback from a lot of people so that lots of input is heard, especially from those affected by the decisions and those who are particularly knowledgeable. This rich information can then be processed and turned into decisions by a circle with a manageable circle size of ideally 4 to 8 people.

The Mission Circle

The General Circle will typically be busy with supporting the day-to-day work. Yet, organizations also need to keep an eye on their long-term wellbeing.

To make sure that the organization is accountable to its overall mission and pays attention to longer-term decisions and strategies, a separate circle holds the mission in its domain: the Mission Circle.

(You can also call it the Purpose Circle, Anchor Circle, the board, Elder Circle, Wisdom Circle, ...)

The Mission Circle will ideally have members from outside the organization so fresh and new ideas can flow into the organization.

As usual, the Mission Circle is double linked with two people being part of Mission Circle and of the General Circle.

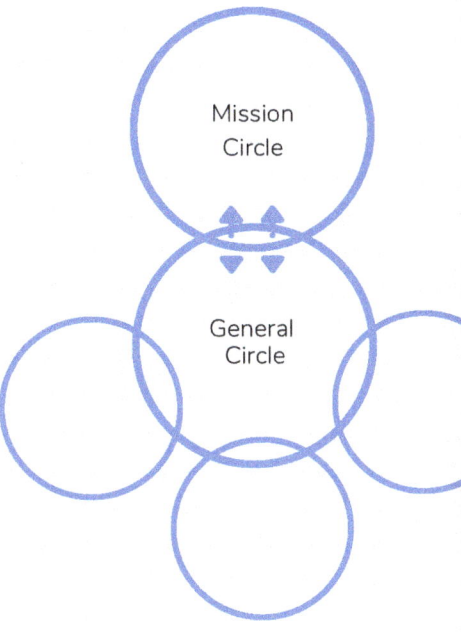

Tips and tricks

When it comes to circle structure, the most common misconception is that power 'should' be centralized. Yet, with the clarity of aims and domains, it is not necessary to create one powerful center, and it's much more resilient and enjoyable to spread authority and responsi-bility throughout the organization.

One challenge in decentralized organizations is that information between circles has to flow well; good reporting by links, transparent and open meeting minutes and proactive feedback as well as curated information to all members becomes even more important than in centralized organizations.

Young organizations often form too many circles and get stretched too thin, or they form too few circles and meet in large groups that don't use their time well because they are not focused enough.

Finding the right fit of roles, circles, and information flow is a "dance" that takes some practice!

The Sociocratic Selection Process

The selection process

The most common use of the selection process is to select people into roles, so we will focus on those. There are other uses of the selection process in the later part of this booklet.

In order to select people into roles, the roles have to exist. It's like one can only put things into boxes if the boxes are built!

Why not simply vote?

Most of us are used to voting — if more than half (or a supermajority) votes for one candidate, that person gets elected and gets the role.

Yet, it can easily happen that someone gets the most votes simply because candidates #2 and #3 divide the votes.

Or it could be that a divisive winning candidate wins although the runner-up #2 would have actually been acceptable to everyone.

Ranked-choice voting and other options are good tweaks to limit the harm - yet in small groups like working circles, there are better alternatives that work without counting votes in the first place!

Voting can easily polarize people on issues and can lead to a competitive win-or-lose mindset.

The sociocracy selection process rewards team players and balanced views on topics.

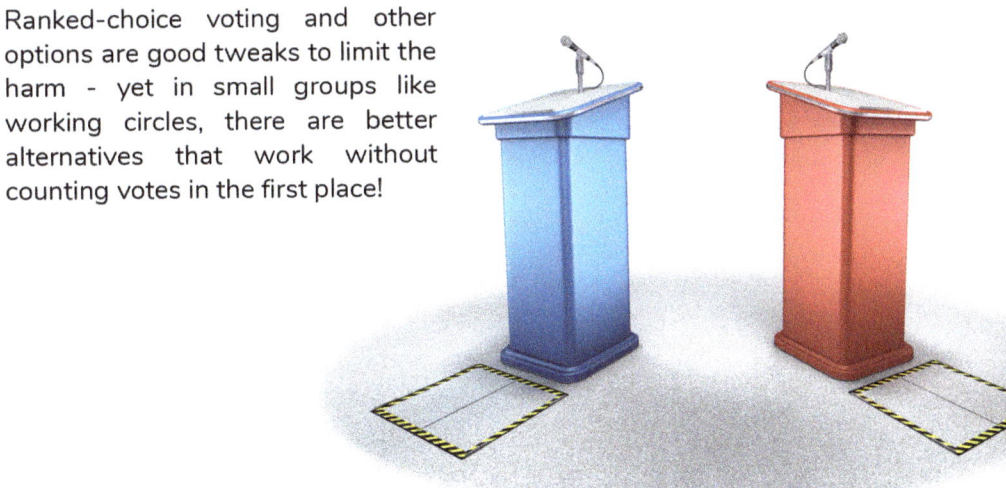

Three phases

Selection are a simple 3-process with a few sub-steps.

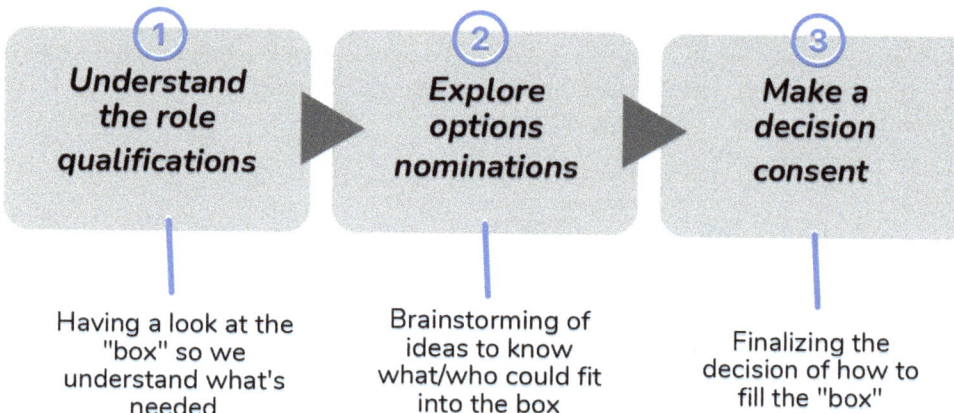

① Understanding the role

What is the role you're filling?
- If there is a role description, we re-read it to make sure we understand it (assuming we've approved the role itself already).
- If there is no role description (like often for circle roles like the facilitator), we describe it verbally.

We make list of qualifications that we'd like to see in the person in the role. (Rounds work well for that!)

We make sure to consent to the list to make sure everyone is good with the criteria

② Exploring the options

The group now explores who might be a good fit for the role.

Nomination
Everyone thinks for a moment who they'd like to nominate. People can also self-nominate.

Nomination round
In a round, everyone shares who they nominated and why.

Change round
In another round, everyone gets an opportunity to change their nomination.

③ Propose a candidate and find consent

The facilitator now proposes a candidate based on the nominations (or asks someone else to make the proposal). In the proposal, the facilitator also determines the term for which the person would fill the role.

The circle will now see if everyone in the circle consents to this candidate. If there is consent, the person is elected into the role.

As always, if there are objections, they get integrated.

Common objections and integrations

There are a lot of options!

- "XX doesn't have enough experience"
    - provide more practice or training
    - shorten the term
    - nominate someone else
- "XX doesn't have enough time"
    - shorten the term
    - free them up (give other responsibilities to someone else)
    - split the role in a meaningful way
    - ...

Benefits and challenges

Most people appreciate how affirming the process is. It's often a sweet feedback moment of appreciation.
Yet, for some people, it is unfamiliar and uncomfortable to speak about each other in front of each other, even if it's positive.
Some also struggle if they are nominated or if they are not nominated.

In our experience, any discomfort fades over time as the team builds trust with each other and the process.

Selection processes for other than roles

Roles and people are not the only way to use the selection process. It can be used for any situation where we have to choose among possible options.

When you can use the selection process:

- Selecting a theme or a venue for a conference
- Selecting a money amount we donate or an amount we charge for a certain offering
- Selecting what book to read in a book club
- Selecting activities into time slots

The qualifications in those cases sound different from qualifications for people in roles. For example: "can be reached by public transportation," "affordable," "social justice topic," or "can be done by all age groups."

You can even use the selection process to select topics into a sorted list of priorities!

Tips and tricks

When it comes to nominations, sometimes people say things like "well, I AM not going to be the leader because I am so bad at it". This is sad and can close doors too early. We've seen many people who are able and willing to step into leadership positions when they get nominated for good reasons and affirmed.

To avoid that people take themselves out of the equation too early, we encourage people to speak who they do nominate, not who they don't nominate.

What's a 'good' meeting?

Meetings are often dreaded. They can take a long time, they can be frustrating and sluggish.
But it doesn't have to be that way! Sociocratic meetings are often faster and more efficient than "ordinary" meetings — and more fun!
This booklet will walk you through the different tools and steps.

A good meeting is
- Effective and efficient: it leads you to outcomes you want to have; within a time frame that's reasonable.
- Connecting: the team trusts each other and feels safe with each other.
- Inclusive: every team member's voice is heard.

Basic meeting format

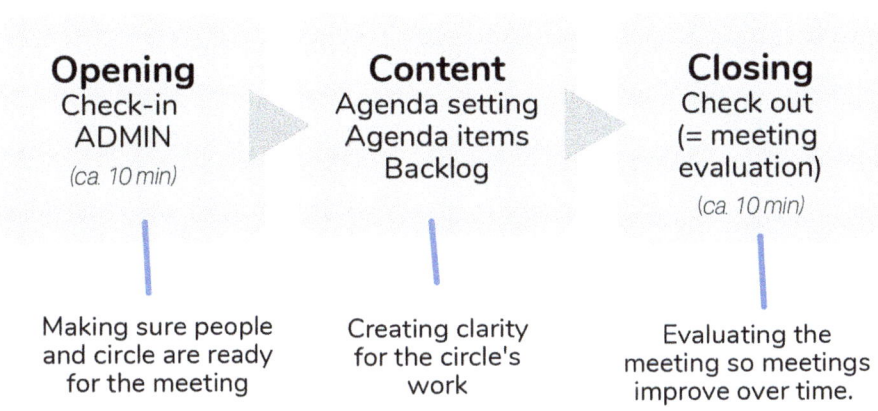

Opening: Check in

We start the meeting as human beings. Let people arrive with each other letting everyone, one by one, do a check-in as **the check-in round**.

People share how they are doing, maybe a little context from their lives.

The more we share, the more we can be three-dimensional human beings. Showing our human side will make it easier to be empathetic, to support each other, be allies to each other - we all come with a story, and what happens around us might affect our meetings directly or indirectly.

Opening: ADMIN

Make sure everyone and everything is ready for the meeting with this checklist:

 Attendance: Who is present? Who is missing? Who is writing notes?

 Duration: How long is this meeting? Does anyone have to leave early?

 Minutes: Are our prior meeting minutes up to date, approved and shared or stored?

 Information: Is there anything else people want to share, like an announcement?

 **N**ext meeting: Is there a next meeting date? If not, is there a plan on when and how the circle is coming to a next meeting date?

Content: Consent to agenda

Before we can jump into the meeting content, we need to make an agreement on what topics we will be talking about, what we are hoping to achieve on each topic, and how long we think that will take.

If someone prepared a proposed agenda, we review it to make sure everyone can give informed consent, and then we accept the agenda by consent. If there are objections to the agenda, we integrate them until we have consent.

- Present the proposed agenda and answer all questions
- Ask for consent from everyone on the agenda and integrate objections

Possible objections
- "XYZ has to leave early, can we switch the order so she can be here for this item?"
- "This agenda is too full, we have to make choices."
- "Agenda item xyz is not within our domain."

Content: Agenda items

Now comes the content part of the meeting.

- In reports, someone gives information about something everyone in the circle needs to know, and then people can ask questions to make sure the information is understood.
- In explorations, there is typically a question or an issue. Someone describes what that question or issue is, and then we explore in rounds our reactions or ideas. Sometimes that's all that's needed.
- If a decision is needed, we make that decision by consent. That means a decision is made when no circle member objects.

Rounds. If you attend a sociocratic meeting, you will notice that a lot of the talking happens in rounds: people talk one by one.

We do that to make sure ...
- everyone gets to speak (not only a few)
- people listen to each other (instead of interrupting each other)
- we always know what we're talking about

Content: Backlog

Often, new topics come up during a meeting. We try to focus on the issue at hand but note down the new issue and write it onto our backlog.

The backlog is then used to plan the next agenda. That way, all meetings follow a common thread, and we keep our shared aim in mind.

Closing: Check-out (meeting evaluation)

Way too often, people just roll their eyes about a meeting and move on to the next thing in their day. While that is understandable, the problem is this: the following meetings will be the same!

We can improve our meetings - and our ways to collaborate overall - if we create a healthy feedback culture. Meeting evaluations are a great place for that!

You can comment on

- **Process**

    (time management, taking turns, facilitation)

- **Content of the meeting**

    (a decision made that you're happy with, or an issue that worries you)

- **Interpersonal dynamics**

    (how connected did you feel? Anything you need to share to leave with integrity?)

Agenda planning

A meeting can work without a planned agenda, as long as the group makes an agreement in the step "Agenda setting" before they start diving into topics.

Yet, a prepared agenda often helps be more intentional about how we move forward through our topics. It only takes a few minutes to avoid spinning our wheels as a group!

The proposed agenda is prepared by the facilitator or leader, or someone else in the group. Then the group can modify if there are objections.

The proposed agenda will include agenda topics from the backlog - the living document holding future agenda items.

If we notice during a meeting that we need to shift gears (for example, we don't consent easily, a new and more important topic comes up, or we run out of time) then the agenda can be adjusted on the fly - with everyone's consent.

Writing proposals

One of the most powerful moments is when a group tackles a complex issue, explores and listens well, solves it together, and then approves the decision with wholehearted consent.

Proposals are a good ways to focus our energy and attention and get specific - and it's that clarity that unleashes action and forward motion. Before there's a proposal on the table, groups are often just bouncing around, exploring this, weighing that.

Where do proposals come from?

In our experience, co-created proposals are the best! Everyone puts their heads together, and the final result is a blend of everyone's best thinking.

Yet, in many situations, it can make sense for a proposal to not be co-created but developed and written up by one person who has the energy to move the issue forward. In that case, the circle would need to process the proposal in a regular consent process.

It's good practice to ask for a lot of feedback early in the process. You can ask for input on each step along the way.

Writing proposals together

What problem are we trying to solve?

After we understand the issue, we generate a proposal in 3 steps

1. **Understanding the scope of solutions**
   Dimensions

2. **Exploring proposal ideas**
   Proposal shaping

3. **Synthesizing proposal ideas**
   Turn into one proposal

We use the consent process to approve the proposal

Approve the proposal

① Understanding the scope: dimensions

Dimensions
What are we going to do about...

- different membership categories
- membership fee
- onboarding
- who can be a member? (requirements)
- ...

When a group is eager to brainstorm ideas to solve a problem, they often get caught up in details too soon.

For more thorough proposals, we start with a list of all the considerations we have to keep in mind to solve the problem. We think of them as headlines we need to elaborate on.

For example, if we want to define the membership and membership processes in an organization, this list shows some of the dimensions.

② Exploring ideas: proposal shaping

The next step is to write down specific ideas for each headline or dimension.

Dimensions
What are we going to do about...
- different membership categories
- membership fee
- onboarding
- who can be a member? (requirements)
- ...

Proposal ideas
I think we should...
- have working and supporting members
- charge $100 membership fee
- Onboarding: sign the value and code of conduct; fill out membership form
- membership limited to people in Hampshire County

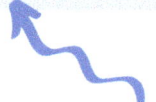

It's ok to expand or contradict proposal pieces by adding our own. Don't discuss, just collect and list them.

③ Synthesizing proposal ideas

Dimensions
What are we going to do about...
- different membership categories
- membership fee
- onboarding
- who can be a member? (requirements)
- ...

Proposal ideas
I think we should...
- have working and supporting members
- charge $100 membership fee
- Onboarding: sign the value and code of conduct; fill out membership form
- membership limited to people in Hampshire County

Proposal
There are 2 membership categories: working and supporting members. The membership fee is $100/year. All members need to live in Hampshire County. To join, a prospective member submits the membership form and signs the value statement and the code of conduct.

One person or a small group now distills the proposal ideas into one proposal.
The proposal can be checked for consent now!

Role descriptions

As mentioned earlier, roles are clusters of tasks and responsibilities that are typically held by one person in the circle. The role description specifies what the role entails.

Roles can be focused on the circle's process (like the role of a facilitator) or on operations (like the Membership Onboarding Manager).

Most typically, a role description is written and approved by the circle. Then a person is selected into the role by consent, often using the selection process.

Earlier, we described roles as a "box" that we then fill with a person. Sometimes, roles are also described as "hats" that one can wear or pass on.

Writing role descriptions

Writing role descriptions works like writing other proposals - even simpler because most dimensions are always the same:

Dimensions
What are we going to do about...
- activities
- pay?
- hours per week
- performance metrics
- workflows/guidelines
- ...

Proposal ideas
I think the role holder should...
- Orient new members and make sure all documents are signed; reach out to potential members
- $25/hour
- 10h/week
- 10 new members/week
- onboarding workflow; membership requirements

People might propose different proposal ideas that still need to be synthesized into a role description.

Tips and tricks

We can move topics through our processes by using this cycle:
- Meeting #1: bring up an issue and surface all the information about the topic. ("What problem are we trying to solve?")
- Meeting #2: brainstorm ideas on the topic and come up with dimension and proposal ideas.
- Between meetings #2 and #3, someone writes up the proposal ideas into a proposal.
- Meeting #3: use the consent process on the proposal (present the proposal, quick reactions and consent/objections)

With this pacing, everyone has time to think together making good use of meeting time and time between meetings. Of course, groups might also go through the whole process in one go!

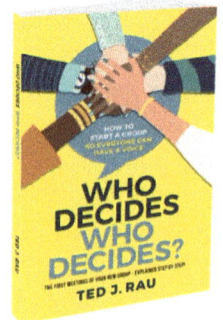

Do you find this step-by-step template useful? See the book *Who Decides Who Decides* for templates on how to start a group!

Feedback and performance

We come together in organizations to work towards a shared aim in support of a mission we're passionate about. What good would all the work we do be if what we're doing isn't working? Taking our own aims seriously also means taking our performance seriously. And that means we need to evaluate whether our actions are effective.

This is true on all levels:
- on the microlevel: we evaluate meetings
- project evaluations (like after holding an event)
- role performance reviews after one year, or policy reviews after 2 years...
- ... or for an aim review every few years.

Why does feedback matter?

Even with the best plans, things often don't quite work out as imagined. With more uncertainty and complexity inside and outside of our organizations, our plans become less likely to become a perfect reality.

Consent decision-making is pragmatic and biased towards action because only action lets us learn how our plans play out in reality. Instead of trying to predict and control future outcomes, we make decisions that give us information on outcomes. Then we continue from there.

The mindset of consent as good-enough-for-now-and-safe-enough-to-try comes in a package deal with evaluating performance and improving what we decide over time. We can't predict the future but we can shift our strategy, track feedback and adjust as needed.

Lead - do - measure

Sociocracy uses a common frame:

1. make plans (lead)
2. carry out the plans (do)
3. evaluate the outcomes (measure)

Most groups and organizations are great at making plans and often focused on carrying out their plans. It's very common that they don't put enough energy into evaluation and reflection — like flying with your eyes closed!

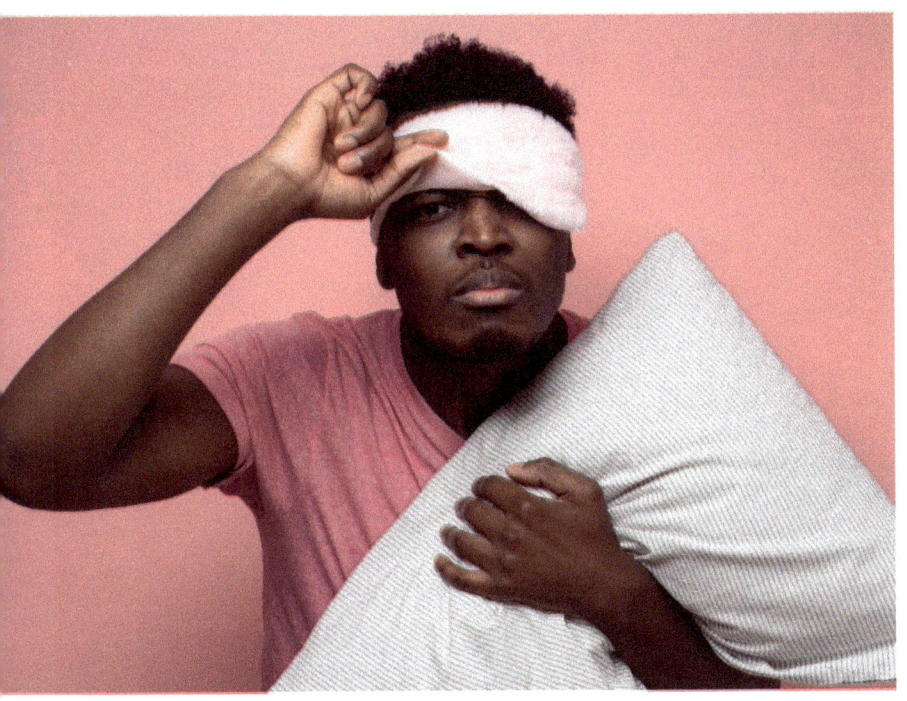

Feedback vs. decision-making

In sociocracy, we try to keep circle sizes to ~4-8 people. Those circle members are the decision-makers in their circle's domain. But that doesn't mean only those 4-8 people can give input on a decision. If a circle commits to taking in feedback from outside of the circle, they can potentially hear thousands of people's input.

Getting feedback comes in many forms. Circles can put out surveys, send out drafts, invite people to their meetings, attend a stakeholders' gathering, read and write in online forums.

The more feedback they hear, the better their decisions will be.

Feedback moments

In everyday life, it's easy to skip evaluations because we get too busy.

To improve our own accountability by evaluating feedback, sociocracy builds "feedback moments" into our workflows and standard processes. That way, feedback has a place and time.

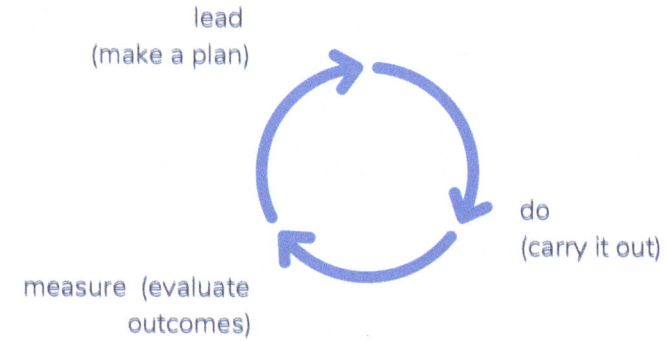

- Meeting evaluations at the end of every meeting
- Policy reviews for every policy, workflow, and role. (Every policy has a term end to enforce evaluation of the policy.)
- Performance reviews for people in roles
- Selection processes (feedback given in nominations)
- Aim reviews

Circle accountability

All the different parts of the feedback cycle depend on accountability. For example, if we integrate an objection by saying that we will evaluate a certain practice in 4 weeks, then this evaluation actually has to happen. Dates, metrics, and follow-ups need to be tracked.
The culture of paying attention to feedback therefore heavily depends on good systems and commitment to the culture and processes.

Personal feedback

The importance of feedback also carries over to personal relationships. How? Imagine someone has a habit of talking very fast working with someone who is hard of hearing. Between them, some information might get lost.

The point here is not to find out who is at "fault" — very often, everyone involved is contributing to a non-ideal pattern. The important thing is to share those observations or concerns so we can work out how issues can be avoided.

Sociocracy itself doesn't prescribe how to communicate; yet, since sociocracy values effectiveness, any way to communicate that makes it more likely to be heard and understood improves communication. Good listening and the ability to express things without blame are key here.

Performance reviews and circle reviews

Performance reviews help us be intentional about giving high-quality feedback to a person in a role.

In a performance review, a group is assembled that is able to provide a 360° assessment of a given focus person's performance - oftentimes from several circles where that focus person holds a role. In the end, the assessment circle and the focus person need to approve the improvement plan.

Other processes

- Performance reviews for a whole team. Same process, just that the focus is the whole circle
- Circle reviews: every member of a circle gives feedback to every member.

understanding the role(s) + performance
What is this person asked to do?
What has been working well/not so well?

▶ **drafting improvement plan**

areas of improvement?
specific ideas to work on?

▶ **consent to the improvement plan**

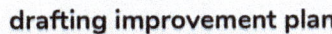

Tips and tricks

In our mainstream culture, blame-free feedback is rare - most of us still have lots to learn in this area. If giving honest personal feedback seems intimidating or even impossible, it is worth having a look at complementary techniques like Nonviolent Communication, Clean Language or Imago.

Nonviolent Communication, for example, helps us uncover and name what's underneath our feelings so it can be shared in a universal language of needs. Thanks to the effectiveness and efficiency of needs consciousness, NVC provides a shortcut in understanding and empathy for oneself and for others.

Books (full books)

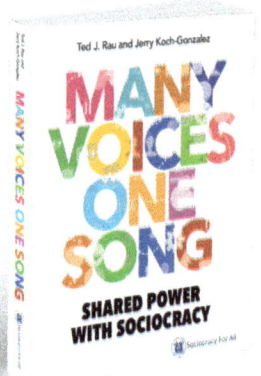

The manual about sociocracy. Packed with information, examples, diagrams and an index. Find deeper explanations about all the processes and situations.

A simple step-by-step guide for starting a group sociocratically. Best for groups 2-12 people.

Educators and parents!
Use sociocracy with children to teach responsible and caring decision-making.

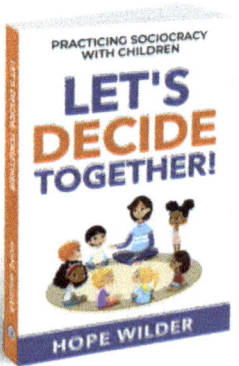

www.sociocracyforall.org/books

Small booklets in this series

For facilitators
(70 pages)

A summary for role holders (70 pages)

>> www.sociocracyforall.org/books

Cards

Bored with your closing rounds? Try out our card decks of check-out prompts!

They include feedback on
- process
- content
- interpersonal

www.sociocracyforall.org/cards

Sociocracy For All

Sociocracy For All is a member-run nonprofit that offers training and consulting for individuals and groups at all levels.

Topics:
- Decision-making by consent
- Organizational structure
- Inclusive meetings
- Performance and accountability

- Facilitation practice
- Immersion programs
- Conflict resolution
- Nonviolent Communication for meeting facilitation
- Certification programs

See our training offerings: www.sociocracyforall.org/training

Offerings

Facilitation
We can facilitate your Board retreat, performance reviews, strategic planning process, conflict engagement, any team that is having a difficult time, or just model and run a sociocratic meeting.

Organizational Structure Redesign
We can help you redesign your organizational structure to better implement sociocracy or to adapt to changing circumstances.

Organizational Audit
We can assess the quality of your current functioning, suggest an improvement plan, and help you carry it out, even if you are not already a sociocratic organization.

Implementing Sociocracy
We can support you from the beginning to the end of the process of adopting sociocracy.

www.sociocracyforall.org/coaching

www.ingramcontent.com/pod-product-compliance
Lightning Source LLC
Chambersburg PA
CBHW061804070526
44586CB00023B/2712